# ESCAPE
# from
# INSANITY,
# ILLUSIONS
# and
# Lies

In this revealing look at A Course
in Miracles, discover the plan to
escape the world of illusions to live
the life we were meant to live and
love it.

## ED GREEN, LC SW

**https://www.insanityillusionslies.com**

Paperback ISBN: 978-1-5136-5679-3

# DEDICATION

I dedicate this book to:

God, my creative source and inspiration

Cindy, for the love, inspiration, contributions and support in completing this work

Toni, beloved daughter who gifted me with the ACIM supplements

Tina, other beloved daughter for her love, help and support

Teah, sometimes little sister sometimes big sister, but all the time a good friend, dedicated to Fresh Start Therapeutic Services in which she included me from the beginning.

Reverend Howard Caesar for his direction and support.

Claudia Olmos of Olmos Design for a fantastic book cover.

John Hodgkinson, owner of Meta Home Publishing Company whose mentorship and guidance helped make this book possible.

And to all you readers out there in hopes that this book makes a positive difference in the quality of your relationships and life.

Escape from Insanity, Illusions and Lies

# TABLE OF CONTENTS

## Preface

What I'm about to reveal to you is the greatest illusion of all time. An illusion so captivating, so compelling, so believable that it seems real. So real that you believe it is real.

And once it becomes real for you it can ensnare you like an insect trapped in a spider's web, you can see no way out and it becomes a prison, a prison from which there appears to be no escape.

***Yet all these things, however real they may seem, are but illusions*** (1)

This is from A Course in Miracles (ACIM).

I call this place, this prison, The Land of Insanity, Illusions and Lies, for short the land of IIL (For our purpose here, pronounced ILL and you'll learn why later).

The Course goes on to tells us that,

***This does not appear to be the case, for the manifestations of this world seem real indeed*** (2)

The land of IIL is the world we live in, from which

there appears to be no escape. The good news is, there's a plan in place to aide us in our escape. This plan can be found in the Course in Miracles, the inspiration for this book.

The Course in Miracles was first published in 1976 and includes a text, workbook, teacher's manual and the supplements; the Song of Prayer, and Psychotherapy: Purpose, Process and Practice pamphlet completed in 1975. The focus here will specifically be on the Psychotherapy: Purpose, Process and Practice pamphlet.

One of the reasons Helen Schucman was chosen to scribe the Course in Miracles was that she was a psychologist and the course clearly states that, *while it was written extensively for psychotherapists, all readers can benefit from its teachings.*

Because Helen was a psychologist was one of the reasons the ACIM became of particular interest to me, and how it came about. I felt having some insight into Helen's life would produce some additional understanding and perspective about the ACIM, the impact it had on her, others around her and the difference it made in her life.

As the story goes, as written on the Light of Christ Truth website, Dr. William Thetford hired Helen to work as a Professor of Medical Psychology at Columbia-Presbyterian Medical Center in New York City in 1958. Their relationship was turbulent, and they clashed constantly.

Their department was filled with competition and hostility between coworkers. There were a lot of scenes of strife and competition, despite the fact that all of them were psychologists. One day Bill, dreading a staff meeting and the typical conflict involved, especially between he and Helen, suggested to Helen before the meeting that "There must be another way."

In Helen's agreeing with Bill, it is believed this "peace" agreement led to the birth of ACIM. Over the next few months Helen experienced a series of dreams and psychic experiences. She had dreams of a large book that was somehow "her" book. She then began having mental conversations with a voice she identified as Jesus. She began asking questions to this "Jesus" about her life, and about Bill's, then she wrote down the answers. Sharing this with Bill led to their collaboration in the production of the ACIM that became a focused goal for them both.

Helen was known for being overtly critical, judgmental, very controlling at times and had many fears and paranoias while Bill had a more passive aggressive personality.

Helen seemed to be able to identify her fears, describing how she was not at peace with this process, as it brought up fears that disturbed her, one being the fear for her own sanity (3).

In a statement by Helen, that can be found on the Foundation for Inner peace website, she says, 'I think the thing that I found upsetting about it was that it went against everything I believe, which is very hard to do (4).'

Ken Wapnick, who had a significant role in editing and publishing ACIM with Helen and knew her well says, 'throughout her life Schucman had a contentious relationship with religion. Schucman desperately wanted to portray herself as a rational, scientific atheist, in keeping with her professional status as a practicing psychologist. At one point she even described herself as a "virulent atheist" (Wapnick 1991:115). The conflict between Schucman's self-conception as a rational scientist and what she experienced with the revelation of the course continued unreconciled throughout her life. Towards the end of her life, she said about the Course: "I know it's true. I just don't believe it" (Wapnick 1991:173).'

Because of this, it caused Helen tremendous conflict stemming from her experience with ACIM that she never reconciled. She knew the course, as you would expect, but she chose not to practice or share its teachings.

When examining the strife, hostility and conflict in describing her working relationships with her colleagues, and Helen's response to it, we can see it was contrary to what she scribed in the ACIM, Psychotherapy: Purpose, Process and Practice pamphlet. In the pamphlet fear, along with its two primary derivatives, anger and guilt were identified as the source of illusions. These emotions were also prominent in the relationships described above in which she identifies throughout the ACIM as imprisoning us by the illusions promoted by these emotions. Ironically enough, ACIM tells us it is precisely these emotions that gives rise to the illusions we must escape. As a psychotherapist, having seen how this played out over the years in people's lives, I've come to view fear, anger and guilt as a model provided us by ACIM for understanding the human condition brought about by the illusions of this world along with a plan to escape them.

I discuss in chapter 2, how the psychotherapy pamphlet emphasizes recognition of this model (fear, anger and guilt) that imprisons us as the first of 7 steps in escaping illusions. Helen's colleagues were her jailers, sustaining hers, as well as their captivity, by way of conflict. By not recognizing the relationships as the means of escape made the illusions real, evidenced by their conflicts. This is the basis of the second of 7 steps that she also writes about in the psychotherapy pamphlet and discussed in chapter 4. It's like what she says; "I know it's true. I just don't believe it" and what she writes in the psychotherapy pamphlet; "*Illness is therefore a mistake and needs correction. And as we have already emphasized, correction cannot be achieved by first establishing the "rightness" of the mistake and then overlooking it* (5)," are at odds.

She knew it to be true, yet rejected it, therefore, either unaware of the connection of what she wrote to her peer relationships, which seems unlikely, or was aware and chose not to apply it. Either way, because she made a choice, she took no real responsibility for the adversarial quality of the relationships with her peers. This is the fourth step discussed in chapter 5. Recognizing the importance of our relationships as a vehicle in which the process of forgiveness can take place. Without that, forgiveness, that she writes about extensively throughout the ACIM, prevented her reconciling her past and removing blocks ('Helen was known for being overtly critical, judgmental and very controlling at times') that kept her from having more positive and productive relationships with her peers. I believe this is what Ken Wapnick spoke of when he said; *She knew the course, as you would expect, but she chose not to practice it, resulting in a painful death.* In contrast to this was Bill Thedford who did practice it and lived a joyous life. (6)

One can conclude the contrast between the two demonstrates the benefit from the study of ACIM. However, there are other conclusions that can be drawn. At that time, spirituality and mental health issues were kept separate compared to today where recognizing our spiritual nature is gaining more and more acceptance when treating mental health problems. This could very well be the reason that even though she was a psychologist, and wrote *"As all therapy is psychotherapy, so all illness is mental illness* (7)*,"* she was unable to apply this to her life and to escape the prison she created for herself. However, in her writings Helen showed us how we can recognize the illusions that become our prison, the model, and the next steps to escape that she didn't embark on that are written of in the pages ahead.

Psychotherapist and other mental health professionals who understand the value of addressing the spiritual nature of those seeking their help or guidance may find this look into Helen's life a useful perspective. The fact that Helen declared herself an atheist was of little consequence from what I can tell because we're told, "*To be a teacher of God, it is not necessary to be religious or even to believe in God to any recognizable extent. It is necessary, however, to teach forgiveness rather than condemnation* (8)."

However, what is significant in these accounts written about Helen, is that they don't include forgiveness, an important spiritual principal, emphasized throughout the ACIM and discussed in chapter 5. Knowing this to be the case, it was a choice Helen made to not apply the ACIM teachings, including forgiveness, to her own life. This can be viewed as her choosing condemnation over forgiveness, as demonstrated in her relationships with her peers.

What Helen has shown us though is that, the ACIM can serve as another way to better understand our worldly experience as spiritual beings without the dogma of traditional religion, while accommodating the psychotherapy methodologies of choice, and training.

The format and applications of principles here can be

used regardless of religious belief or therapeutic methods once there's an agreed upon goal or outcome that blends psychotherapy and religion (in a spiritual sense of the meaning) discussed in chapter 6.

As psychotherapists, as well as many others of us, can recognize the outward behavior of someone is an expression of an internal condition.

Although this book is written from a psychotherapist's perspective, as another viewpoint for psychotherapist, for students of A Course in Miracles, and anyone really, who wants insight into their spiritual nature having a human experience. This book will introduce a framework and fresh perspective of the ACIM based on the Psychotherapy: Purpose, Process and Practice pamphlet that can serve as a format to further enhance the study and understanding of the ACIM to aide in our spiritual growth.

The ACIM is consistent in its teachings about there being only two mental conditions, or emotions, Love and fear and we all have experienced both and sometimes became the source of mental distress when the experience is not one of love.

When Love is absent, we deny our true self, our spiritual nature, and fear is allowed to enter. Fear is the source of illusions that can trap and imprison us.

This causes us to feel like the world is against us and prevents us from living the life we're meant to live. When we don't realize what imprisons us, we don't recognize the need to escape, viewing it as an external, rather than an internal condition.

Others who are not students of ACIM and are searching for a way to understand their human experience, and perhaps a resource to inspire desired changes, will find this a useful perspective organized into an identifiable process. The 7-step format outlined can serve as a guide for those who aren't followers or familiar with ACIM. The interpretations of the ACIM teachings will deliver powerful insights that can be of great value to those seekers of truth and self-discovery.

Not everybody needs or will seek a trained psychotherapist, but most everyone wants to better understand how they can have a richer, fuller and joyful life, and what they can do to bring it forth. This book can be a valuable self-discovery aide for those simply seeking another way to recognize and navigate through this world of illusions to get more out of life.

Because we cannot know the full depth and impact of Helen's experience with the ACIM that caused her to not receive the gift that she presented to us, we can't really judge the choices she made, but we can learn from them and decide for ourselves based on what she left us. For me this includes the inspiration for this book.

I have been a long-time seeker of a deeper understanding of ACIM core principles and how they can be applied in relationships. The Psychotherapy:

Purpose, Process and Practice pamphlet summarizes the ACIMs teachings, as well as, includes a plan as a means for escape. I envisioned a process that leads from the escape of illusions that hold us back, to leading the life we were meant to live. This process precedes what I call a **P**erception **C**hanging **E**xperience or **E**vent (PCE).

The case examples presented to illustrate this process, are real. Only their names have been changed to protect their identity and confidentiality. They are also meant to illustrate what can occur in each step to give you, the reader, a sense of progression and interpersonal interactions from the first to last step starting with; becoming aware of illusions as the source of our distress, an identifiable process to facilitate change, leading to a perception changing event or experience (PCE), causing a shift in perception revealing the illusion, creating the opportunity to decide differently. The case examples are also used to demonstrate a therapeutic model, how it can be used and that it's not exclusive to mental health professionals, or organized religion or what we've come to know as traditional psychotherapy, when it comes to escaping illusions.

This book is my attempt to present how the ACIM teachings that emphasize, we are first spiritual beings, but our human thought system blocks our awareness of this and is the cause of our earthly struggles. I also wanted to show that the process provided to bring this to our awareness I consider neither religious or clinical, but therapeutic. This is the value I want the case examples to demonstrate and hope I'm affective in doing so because the plan, that can be found in the ACIM from which these 7 steps evolve, as you will discover, is for all.

I'm going to share this plan with you, and based on the pamphlet's teachings, how the plan works, who carries it out, the 7 step process, and the PCE, that will lead from escape from imprisonment to freedom. This is the Miracle we are all looking for. Right?

Love. In the end, that's what awaits us. The realization we came from Love, forgot and imprisoned ourselves in the Land of IIL. Only when we become aware that we need to and can escape the distress of this place and return to Love, and realize we cannot do it alone, we can understand we can live the life we want to live and Love it. My intention is to show you this is what God's plan is all about as presented in the ACIM. You'll see that there is a process involving steps that leads from the insanity, illusions and lies of this world, to the Perception Changing Experiences/Events (PCEs) revealing your true nature, hidden no more by illusions, and how this is the source of Miracles.

# Introduction

I've been a psychotherapist for many years. After receiving my license in the early 80s I was introduced to the Course in Miracles. This happened after my first divorce and I met a woman, Mary, who gifted me with a book called Loving Relationship by Sondra Ray, published in 1980. In the first chapter, 'Clear up your relationship with God,' I read; 'What is God? God is Love.'

This was a remarkable discovery for me. I had never seen or heard this expressed quite like it was in this book. The first question that flashed across my mind was, why didn't anybody tell me about this before? They probably did, I'm almost certain, but not in a way that made sense to me as did this, because this was not the God I grew up learning about.

I recall my mother insisting on me going to our small community Baptist Church on Sundays where she was the organist. I remember the minister being a stocky, built man with big hands and thick stubby fingers. When he made a fist, he looked like Wreckit Ralph as he moved about the pulpit, jumping up and down, yelling and pounding on the podium preaching the message we were born sinner and there was nothing we could do about it. We had to repent right now or risk burning in hell. Made worst was, being told God knows all and sees all, which meant, there was nowhere to run, and nowhere to hide. I was doomed. To me as a young boy this was pretty scary. So up till I read the book, Loving Relationships, I really didn't get involved with religious matters or concerns. If somebody asked if I believed in God, I said yes, as expected and hoped there were no questions.

'God is Love' was a new and different way to look at God and was reinforced when Mary invited me to Unity Church of Houston for the first time. The message was the same, God is Love, Love is God. When I went into the Unity book store there was book after book not only saying, reinforcing and supporting the same thing, there were many other books that sparked my interest. I was introduced to metaphysics that spread to quantum physics that began to expand my understanding of Love and our spiritual nature that had a scientific appeal. After all, my degree is a Master of Science in Social Work. So, there I was, a college graduate with a master's degree, a Navy veteran and just now coming to this awareness. I began to awaken. To say the least, I became a sponge, reading everything I could get my hands on having to do with ways of understanding God, and Love, and me. Little did I know I was being prepared for what was to come.

One day while looking at books in the Unity bookstore I came across A Course in Miracles.

The first thing that caught my attention was that it was written for psychotherapist. I thought, I'm a psychotherapist and I could use a miracle, so why not.

As I studied the Couse over the years, I came to learn miracles weren't what I thought them to be. As a practicing psychotherapist, I just knew the success I experienced in helping others was due to my skills, methods and uncanny insights. But, over the years I came to learn I could cure no one, but I could help others to heal by learning and continuing to learn, that all healing comes from a Source higher than myself. I began to learn about the nature of miracles, that they naturally occurred and, that they could be summoned.

As I became more involved in the Course, the teachings began to find their way into my therapy work with others, sometimes using the ACIM wording that even surprised me.

It blended amazingly well with psychotherapy schools of thought, theory, applications, methods and techniques.

After years of studying the text, I discovered the supplements. Most appealing was the pamphlet, "Psychotherapy: Purpose, Process and Practice." My daughter actually discovered them and gifted me the supplements on CDs. I listen to them in my truck everywhere I went. It began to organize my thinking of how I understood the ACIM and its teachings as it summarized the course quite brilliantly and began to shift how I thought about psychotherapy. Facilitating this shift was gaining an understanding that was a clear contradiction of those early teachings of God.

Quite baffling, was God's plan for us. People would refer to it, but never really said what it was, or explained, least not in a way that made any sense. Everything that happens to us seemed to come down to, "it's part of God's plan," or something similar, as though our fate, even tragedy, is somehow part of God's Divine plan, which seemed to cover every possible life circumstance. It was very confusing. I don't think those who fall back on this way of thinking to make sense of the world, and their relationship with God, really knew either, so it became for me, just one of those unknowable mysteries. But I figured it wouldn't hurt to try and be as good as I could, just in case, because that was part of God's plan too. And though I might have come across it in the Bible, it never stood out in a way that was understandable to me because of the language, context and my literal interpretation I was taught in those early days. One day it became clear. The plan was right there in the Psychotherapy pamphlet of the ACIM. It wasn't just a plan I could understand, it was an escape plan.

My hope in writing this book is to reveal the simplicity of this plan, the process identified for carrying it out and the role we play to secure our escape and helping others to escape in the name of Love. In the end, that's what awaits us. The realization we came from Love, forgot and imprisoned ourselves in the Land of IIL. Only when we become aware that we need to and can escape the distress of this place and return to Love, and realize we cannot do it alone, we can understand we can live the life we want to live and Love it. My intention is to show you this is what God's plan is all about as presented in the ACIM. You'll see that there is a process involving steps that leads from the insanity, illusions and lies of this world, to the Perception Changing Experiences/Events (PCEs) revealing your true nature, hidden no more by illusions, and how this is the source of Miracles.

# Chapter 1

## The Plan

Before my study of ACIM I never understood what was meant by 'God's Plan.' I would hear people talk about events and circumstances, good or bad, as part of God's Plan. This seemed so random making it very confusing. When I finally read it for myself in the Psychotherapy pamphlet, I was surprised at its simplicity and how easy it was to understand. See for yourself.

**The sacred calling of God's holy Son for help in his perceived distress can be but answered by his father. Yet He needs a voice through which to speak His holy Word; a hand to reach His Son and touch his heart. In such a process, who could not be healed? This holy interaction is the plan of God Himself, by which His Son is saved** (9).

Let's take a closer look at this plan.

*The sacred calling of God's holy Son for help in his perceived distress can be but answered by his father* – As the Course outlines, we are one, appearing to be

1

in separate parts having different experiences, some causing distress, so the purpose is to provide help to those who ask or are in need of help.

*Yet He needs a voice through which to speak His holy Word; a hand to reach His Son and touch his heart. In such a process, who could not be healed?* - Here we see there's a process in which help is given and received and someone to give and receive it on God's behalf.

*This holy interaction is the plan of God Himself, by which His Son is saved*, is the goal, or outcome. Saved by escaping from illusions by becoming aware we are one rather than many, so to help another is to help ourselves succeed and live the life we were all meant to live.

To believe what the ACIM is telling us, we are of one Source and only appearing to be separate and different, is the cause of our distress. The effects of this are illusions that seem real and at times, feel inescapable. Accepting we are of one Source, the simplicity of the plan becomes better understood and appreciated. Recognizing we are connected we become aware that when helping another we help ourselves. This is emphasized throughout the ACIM in the idea that giving and receiving are the same. It's the interactions between us that makes our relationships with others so vital to the success of this plan.

Here it was, God's plan, clear and in a way, I could understand well enough to be helpful to me, useful in psychotherapy, and then perhaps, in workshops, seminars, and relationships important to me. Maybe one day, even write a book.

I'd like to say the contents of the narrative that follows came to me in a flash of understanding. It did not, at least not at first. It took an experience to initiate the process, along with some help, allowing it to unfold.

# Chapter 2

# The Model

A few years ago, a woman, Debbie, came to me, seeking help for depression and anxiety. During the initial evaluation she told me her story. She was in conflict about the recent decision she made to remarry her ex-husband after 10 years of divorce, and was uncertain if she was making the right decision. During the initial evaluation, a routinely asked question was if she wanted to include her religious/spiritual faith or teachings to draw on as an additional strength and support and she said no. We proceeded on from there.

Over the next month what emerged was right from the psychotherapy pamphlet (ACIM/PP) and presented to her in terms of her descriptions and context of the conflict she was experiencing. By this time, I learned, if I just kept quiet, stepped aside, I would be guided, and I was. This is what happened.

On a dry marker board, I wrote the words **fear, anger and guilt,** as they emerged from her story. Fear on the bottom and guilt and anger over top of it, across from each other. Then I drew a line, connecting one to the other forming a closed triangle and wrote her name in the middle. This visual helped her to understand how each influenced the other and began to see why she felt trapped. She was unable to move beyond the boundaries of these emotions she was experiencing that held her captive and were being expressed as depression and anxiety from which she felt there was no escape. She felt her prison. This process, using the dry maker board, led to the first of other PCEs that was a step in her self-discovery, insight into why she felt trapped.

This was not planned or thought out. It just flowed in the course of our discussions. What I came to realize was, this was a model provided to us by ACIM for understanding the human condition brought about by the illusions of this world.

A Course in Miracles tells us there are only two emotions, Love and fear. We experience derivatives of each. Derivatives of Love; joy, happiness and peace. Derivatives of fear; anger, guilt, resentment to name a few of each. We'll delve deeper into the aspects of fear later on.

Based on this, I have come to realize when someone comes to a psychotherapist, they are not at peace, they're distressed and asking for help (*The sacred calling of God's holy Son for help in his perceived distress...*) to escape their prison. This brings us back to our model as described in the ACIM Psychotherapy pamphlet.

**Fear** - *No one in this world escapes fear* (10)

**Anger** - *A fundamental error is the belief that anger brings us something we really want and that by justifying attack we are protecting ourselves* (11)

**Guilt** - *What then can illness be except an expression of sorrow and guilt* (12). *Once God's son is seen as guilty, illness becomes inevitable* (13). By the way. This is why I call this place the Land of IIL.

Fundamentally, we're all captors of the illusions of this world. And those held captive by fear want to escape to Love, but all may not be fully awake to this. Those who are awakening will find helpful insights here in their self-discovery when viewed as a prison from which they can escape by freeing themselves from these burdensome emotions and shedding perceived limitations. This is where the plan discussed earlier comes in. It's an escape plan

Like any good escape plan it begins with knowing what your escaping from, with steps leading one to another that will lead to freedom. This escape plan and the process involved with carrying out this plan includes 7 steps.

Step 1 Identify the emotional distress that has become the prison

Step 2 Identify and neutralize the guard's/jailers who would keep you captive

Step 3 Overtake the warden, the one in charge of the whole operation

Step 4 Secure a getaway car

Step 5 Map out your escape route

Step 6 You'll need an expert and experienced getaway driver and guide who you can trust to navigate your escape safely.

Step 7 Know your destination, where you are escaping to.

What follows is a look into each step and how each lead us to the next step and our eventual escape.

# Chapter 3

## Step 1
## Identify the emotional distress that has become our prison

Thanks to Debbie, this model became useful in guiding clients in therapy that I used more and more. This led to creating a workshop I call, **Escape from Insanity, Illusions and Lies,** to assist others in better understanding these internal conditions as internal reactions to the illusions holding them captive, and help them become aware there is a way out.

At the end of that first month, together we reviewed Debbie's progress. She was asked again, during the course of the review, if she wanted to incorporate her religious or spiritual teachings as part of our continued work together. This time she said yes. I told her we'd been doing this all along. She just looked at me and smiled and said, "I know." God, nor religion was ever mentioned, but her spiritual nature seemed to connect with what was taken place. That's why this model is an excellent guide regardless of the clinical and therapeutic methodologies practiced by psychotherapist.

Now, recognizing what imprisoned her could Debbie's journey begin, but she didn't know how on her own. And so it is with many of us. Until we can recognize we are imprisoned can we recognize the need to escape. Once we do, it becomes the great journey that beckons us all.

Recognizing first, that we are trapped by our emotions begins the journey of self discovery and healing. As was the case too, of a 17 year old, Ricky, who blacked out when becoming mad with rage. There have been occasions when this happened that someone got hurt and he didn't remember doing it. Though he would express remorse after, it was another's fault for making him angry. The distortion of his thinking prevented him from discovering the source of the emotions he was experiencing that held him hostage.

Parents can feel trapped, especially parents raising their first child with emotional or behavioral challenges. A while back I saw a young mother who was struggling with her first born, Jeremy, a 6 year old with ADHD. She didn't want to put him on medication, fearful of side-affects, but was at a loss, frustrated and had begun to believe she was a bad mother because she wasn't able to handle Jeremy's hyperactive behavior and intense tantrums. Feeling there was no way out, she feared she would damage her relationship with him by being too hard on him or not hard enough.

Not too long ago I met a lady, Martha, who was experiencing depression as a result of sexual abuse as a child. She recognized and could identify the Fear/Anger/Guilt Model as her prison. Fearing places with a lot of people, she ventured very little from home and it was affecting her relationship with her children, especially her teen age daughter, unaware of how much fear influenced her parenting.

Then there was the 10 year old boy, Carl, whose mother passed away for reasons unknown to him. His family kept the reason for her death from him to protect him. This caused him to be fearful, sensing something was being kept from him. It wasn't just fear trapping him, it was the manifestations of his fear that was really scary for him.

During a workshop, Jimmy shared being depressed months at a time, causing him to feel immobilized and not wanting to do anything or be around anyone. As he learned that depression was an effect and not a cause he could then recognize the feeling of being locked up in a prison and held hostage by his emotions.

All of us have been imprisoned by fear anger and guilt to one degree or another. There've been times, we've all felt trapped by them. You may feel trapped even now but may not recognize your bondage as emotions keeping you connected to the past. Or you may know but feel powerless.

Though we cannot deny our past or what happened, we're told we can put it in perspective.

*He must be willing to reverse his thinking and to understand that what he thought projected its effects on him were made by his projections on the world. The world he sees does therefore, not exist* (14).

We made it up and we're still making it up. A way to view this is simple; the glass is either half full or half empty. Half empty let's say represents a belief of lack, half full, a belief of abundance, when in fact it only has the meaning we give it, which is based on our past learning. That meaning then is the reality we experience, the reality we live.

Like Henry Ford once said, "If you think you can do a thing or think you can't do a thing, you're right." What you think becomes true for you.

I can't say with certainty that how I understand the psychotherapy supplement was because of my background and training as a psychotherapist and study of ACIM, or it was a gift to understand it in the way that I do, so I researched in hopes of learning more and found virtually nothing on the psychotherapy pamphlet that would further my understanding. I discovered very little compared to what was evolving from the work I was doing with others using Fear/Anger/Guilt Model and my continued study of the ACIM and the Psychotherapy pamphlet.

If this work, Escape from Insanity, Illusions and Lies, opens the way to further interpretations of ACIMs psychotherapy pamphlet, perhaps others will take it further and delve deeper to further aide in our understanding and recognition of distress causing illusions to promote more positive, purposeful loving relationships that can only contribute to our spiritual growth.

In fact, the impact on me wasn't entirely clear until sometime after the work with Debbie was done and I continued applying this Fear/Anger/Guilt Model in my practice and workshop development did it evolve and gain further clarity.

The ACIM/PP identifies the prison as fear, anger and guilt holding us captive, those we perceive as our captors, and offers an escape plan that when followed we can free ourselves. This is the model I speak of.

Debbie was imprisoned by fear, anger and guilt. The more I worked with this with others, the more I began to see this as a therapeutic model from which people could benefit by bringing an understanding of their emotional experience viewed from the relationship they have with the external world, while providing them with hope and helping them find a way out. As described in the ACIM/PP;

## Fear

### *No one in this world escapes fear*

In the case of Debbie, her fear was that the same mistakes that have happened in the past would be repeated, so the past was the present.

## Anger
*...the belief that anger brings him something he really wants and that by justifying attack, he is protecting himself*

She was angry with herself because of not speaking out about how she felt, so blamed herself and projected it onto others, at times in angry outbursts.

## Guilt

*What then can illness be except an expression of sorrow and guilt. Once God's son is seen as guilty, illness becomes inevitable.*

Guilt came from doubt that she could be wrong when she was shut down by her ex and was unable to express herself about how much it felt like it did when they were married, causing her an emotional conflict of who was right, her or him, adding anxiety to her depression.

The ACIM/PP makes it very clear we all experience fear. The very fact that we are in this world is proof of this. Anger and guilt are the primary derivatives of fear and can take other forms that can almost always be traced back to one or all of the three. The ACIM identifies other forms fear can take that may not always be obvious.

# The anatomy of Fear

I want to pause here to look closer at what is said about fear, and that, no one escapes it. What is fear that we can't escape it? In researching fear, I looked at a number of sources.

*Fear reaction starts in the brain and spreads through the body to make adjustments for the best defense, or flight reaction. The **fear** response starts in a region of the brain called the amygdala* (15)

*Fear is one of the most basic human emotions. It is programmed into the nervous system and works like an instinct. From the time **we're** infants, **we** are equipped with the survival instincts necessary to respond with **fear** when **we** sense danger or feel unsafe. **Fear** helps protect us* (16).

The sources researched were very consistent in how fear is defined and its origin as an internal response innate to our nature, our biology you could say, to warn and protect us from perceived threats and/or danger to our survival. This is how humankind was able to survive as a species.

Imagine a world where no one experienced fear. There would be no sense of danger or risk. Makes me wonder if mankind would have survived the Stone Age.

Randy Shingler explains.
*A primitive part of the brain, the amygdala, is where it is generally agreed that fear originates and causes responses to events and circumstances. Over millions of years nature has assembled into the*

*amygdala memories of harmful and traumatic events.*

*When the amygdala recognizes footprints of events it perceives as threats it responds by triggering fear within us. It is a conditioned response over which we can have control if we have the will to exercise it. Otherwise it becomes a construct of fear in our minds* (17).

Here we begin to understand why no one in this world escapes fear. It is an ancient function of our brain as Randy explains further.

*There are many different fears that can be accumulated, developed and sometimes transferred to others during the course of a person's lifetime. They become constructs in the depths of the mind.*

Through the evolution of humanity we have been able to minimize the significant, external dangers that would threaten humanity's existence and enable us to thrive as a species. The question that arises from this is, how did God become an external threat to be feared, as many of us were taught, if fear is hardwired into our make up for the purpose of survival?

Eugene H. Merrill in his article, Entry into Fear, based on his research of the Baker's Evangelical Dictionary of Biblical Theology and definitions from International Standard Bible Encyclopedia -Fear, begins to shed some light on this.

*In time, however, fear of God or of manifestations of the divine became a subcategory of fear in general and thus developed a theological signification pervasively attested throughout the Bible. While the normal meaning of fear as dread or terror is retained in the theological use of the terms, a special nuance of reverential awe or worshipful respect becomes the dominant notion. But fear of God also produces fear of wrath and judgment in those who do not know him or who refuse to serve him.*

We see a shift in fear's meaning, evolving into two sides, or perspectives.

On one side;

*In Psalms 90:11 the King James Version has "According to thy fear so is thy wrath," the Revised Version (British and American) "and thy wrath according to the fear that is due unto thee"; the meaning probably is "thy wrath is in proportion to thy fear."*

The "fear of the Lord" is a frequent phrase in Apocrypha, and is highly exalted, e.g. Ecclesiasticus 1:11-30; the idea of it became gradually more and more elevated; in 2:15,16 it is joined with the love of God.

"Fear" is the natural consequence of sin *(Genesis 3:10; 4:13,14; Proverbs 28:1); it comes as a punishment (Deuteronomy 28:25,28). The fear of man and of evils are dangers to be avoided, from which the fear of God delivers (Numbers 14:9; 21:34; Psalms 23:4; 31:14, etc.).*

"Fear" sometimes stands for the object of fear *(Proverbs 10:24; Isaiah 66:4); for the object of worship (Genesis 31:42,53, "the God of Abraham, and the Fear of isaac," pachadh).*

The shift;
Fear of God also lies at the heart of successful living in the world. Wisdom literature makes it
clear that the fear of the Lord is the beginning of wisdom, a fear equated with the "knowledge of the Holy One" ( *Prov 9:10 ; 1:7 ; Psalm 111:10* ). *To fear God is to know him and to know him is to fear him. Such healthy fear enables one to praise God ( Psalm 22:23 ; Rev 14:7 ); to enjoy benefits and blessings at his hand ( Psalm 34:9 ; Psalms 103:11 Psalms 103:13 Psalms 103:17 ); to rest in peace and security ( Psalm 112:7-8 ); and to experience length of days ( Prov 10:27 ; 19:23 ). But fear of God also produces fear of wrath and judgment in those who do not know him or who refuse to serve him. There are, thus, two sides of the fear of the Lord — that which produces awe, reverence, and obedience, and that which causes one to cower in dread and terror in anticipation of his displeasure* (18).

Other sources also tell us that the fear assigned to God is a contradiction from its intended understanding and meaning.

On the other side;

*Some translations of the Bible, such as the New International Version, sometimes replace the word "fear" with "reverence"* (19)

**Fear** *of God refers to* **fear** *or a specific sense of respect, awe, and submission to a deity. People subscribing to popular monotheistic religions might* **fear** *divine judgment, hell or God's omnipotence* (19)

*Proverbs 9:10 says, "The fear of the LORD is the beginning of wisdom, and knowledge of the Holy One is understanding."* Basically, this verse teaches that the fear of God is foundational to true wisdom; all other types of learning are worthless unless built upon a knowledge of the Lord Himself.

For the unbeliever, the fear of God is the fear of the judgment of God and eternal death, which is eternal separation from God *(Luke 12:5; Hebrews 10:31)*. For the believer, the fear of God is something much different. The believer's fear is reverence of God. *Hebrews 12:28-29 i*s a good description of this:

*"Therefore, since we are receiving a kingdom that cannot be shaken, let us be thankful, and so worship God acceptably with reverence and awe, for our 'God is a consuming fire.'"*

This reverence and awe are exactly what the fear of God means for Christians. This is the motivating factor for us to surrender to the Creator of the Universe (20).

The author of Psalm 111, like the author of Proverbs, highly values the fear of the Lord as an incentive to a righteous walk with God *(cf. Ps 111:10; Prov 9:10)*. Qoheleth goes as far as to sum up our entire relationship with God by saying, *"The last word, when all is heard: Fear God and keep his commandments, for this is man's all" (Eccles 12:13)*. In 27 places, the Bible commends the fear of the Lord as something positive, helpful and enabling.

*The fear of the Lord is the beginning of any authentic relationship with God in the same sense that conception is the beginning of life. We begin to live as a person the moment we are conceived in our mother's womb. But our life does not end when we are born and mature. In the same way, fear of the Lord is the beginning, the starting point, the foundation of a right relationship with God. When that right relationship reaches its full measure in heaven, our hearts will be bursting with joy. In the court of heaven, we will be overwhelmed with awe and wonder before the divine majesty of God. Amazed, astonished by his love, we will truly understand that "the fear of the Lord...endures forever" (Psalm 19:9)* (21).

What we see here is, somewhere along the line in humanities evolution, there was a shift in consciousness giving rise to the belief God is a punishing God to be feared, and for those who disobeyed would be punished or struck down and condemned to hell after death. This belief became more and more dominant in our thinking down through the ages. The result of this dual meaning of fear produced confusion brought about by our split mind.

The ACIM says of fear; ***Whenever there is fear, it is because you have not made up your mind. Your mind is therefore split, and your behavior inevitably becomes erratic. Correcting at the behavioral level can shift the error from the first to the second type, but will not obliterate the fear*** (22).

Does this mean the original meaning of fear, self-preservation and the survival of the species, that remains intact, is why no one escapes fear (**the second type**)? And that, '*everyone can reconsider its* (fear) *causes and learn to evaluate them correctly?'* And correctly means that, '*For the unbeliever, the fear of God is the fear of the judgment of God and eternal death, which is eternal separation from God (Luke 12:5; Hebrews 10:31),* is an unreal belief? An illusion?

Follow along with this. The appearance of separation, or the gap between us, is an illusion, according to the ACIM, when in truth we are one and this gap doesn't actually exist. Because we see one another as separate we see one another as something other than who we are to each other and so assign ungodly attributes, complicating our relationships and circumstances.

***For it would mean His Love could harbor just a hint of hate, His gentleness turns sometimes to attack,***

*and His eternal patience sometimes fail. All this do you believe, when you perceive a gap between your brother and yourself. Here is the fear of God most plainly seen. For Love is treacherous to those who fear, since fear and hate can never be apart. No one who hates but is afraid of love, and therefore must he be afraid of God* (23).

Here in may lie the answer to our question. When we do not recognize the source of our oneness, God, because of the illusion of separateness, we fear one another. How can we then fear one another and not fear God? As mentioned earlier, there is only Love or fear and as stated earlier, *God is Love*. Is the answer, then; Fear each other and we fear God? You decide.

Having a better understanding of how and why fear is the root cause of our captivity is important to this discussion. The insanity of illusions brought about by the dual meaning of fear and the illusions that rise from it gives us some insight into the origin of the lie from which they spring and made real.

*Fear cannot long be hidden by illusions, for it is part of them. It will escape and take another form, being the source of all illusions* (24).

It is fear that imprisons us all to some degree or another, and we've all experienced this emotion directly or its various forms and it has either motivated or terrified us. Somewhere in between, fear has prevented many of us from living the life we want.

Fear and it's two primary derivatives, anger and guilt, are not the only forms fear may take. There are many others in ACIM (ACIM / 11.V.9.1.204) that I'm certain you'll recognize.

**Supercilious**
Arrogant, Condescending, Haughty, Pompous, Patronizing, Scornful, Stuck-up

**Distance**
Remote, Isolated, Secluded
**Callous**
Heartless, Unfeeling, Coldhearted, Uncaring, Insensitive, Unsympathetic, Cold, Cruel
**Uninvolved**
Uncomplicated, Easy, Simple, Plain, Detached, Removed
**Unbelieving**
Incredulous, Skeptical, Doubting, Suspicious, Questioning
**Emotionally Shallow**
Petty, Trivial, Small minded, One dimensional
**Desperate**
Frantic, Anxious, Worried, Distressed, Distracted, Fraught, Hopeless

Sometimes we may have felt held hostage by these emotions because we saw no options or choices as our thinking can become that of young children as we think, "She or he made me mad," or "it's his or her fault," perceiving attack, thereby justifying our attack on them, if we allow ourselves to admit it. You may say, these emotions have no walls or bars, strait jackets or chains that could hold a person prisoner.

True. They don't. What holds us prisoner is more powerful than that. The inability to put the past, from where these emotions come, in proper perspective has the power to keep us in a place separated from others and hold us hostage, complete with guards and jailers. This is what makes the name, **Land of insanity illusions and lies** appropriate because we are all imprisoned here together.

In Step 1 We must become aware of our prison by recognizing the emotions that have become our prison, resolve them, put them in the proper perspective, or let them go. One way to do this is recall and write down the most recent situations, people and/or circumstances next to the emotions that best fit, fear, anger and guilt. Is the absence of Love more apparent in these instances? The more apparent it is the more apparent is your prison.

## Chapter 4

### Step 2
### Who are our Jailers and Captors?

Who are the jailers and guards? All those from our past who stood between us and what we want, caused us pain, treated us unfairly, betrayed us and did us wrong. They have prevented us from the happiness, opportunities, and the life we love and deserve to live. Or maybe, they're just the cause of us having a bad day. This is the thinking that we hold onto and in turn, holds us captive in the land of IILs because, it's not our fault. At least, that's what we tell ourselves.

Like with Debbie who discovered, in recalling her mother and father never argued, she came to believe wives had no opinions or anger. Now looking back on her marriage to her ex-husband, he became the jailer to whom she was conflicted about expressing herself.

Though we cannot deny our past or what happened, we're told we can put it in perspective. For us to escape we must learn the source of these emotions, which is almost always people, places or situation from a past that is no more.

What we've learned so far is that our prison is fear and that its main derivatives, anger and guilt are projections from our past superimposed on the present. Our relationships in the present are then influenced by relationships and situation of a past that no longer exist.

In other words, what we see, is what we made up. This is the illusion. So, you can believe what you see, or see what you believe. We create our reality for better or worse, depending on the choices we make.

It's like that old joke. A wife comes home and finds her husband with another woman. He tells her it's not what she thinks. She shouts, "I caught you cheating on me with my own eyes." He challenges her with, "Who you gonna believe, me or your lyin eyes?" Here is the choice. Truth, or illusion? We're faced with choosing between the two on a daily basis.

Those who would hold us captive are those who would manipulate us, we see as preventing our success, or situations we see as out of our control to blame for our circumstances. When this becomes the source of our fear and fear the source of our distress, distress becomes the source of illusions. In our dealings with the world around us, it's when we no longer feel at peace.

This happens when we react to what someone did or said that triggers negative memories from our past. They become responsible for the hurt we feel now and we treat them that way because they have become a threat to our wellbeing, maybe even our survival when driven by fear. We must see them for who they really are to neutralize them by recognizing they're just as imprisoned as we and may not always ask for help in a way we can understand, as we all sometimes do when fear, anger or guilt decide for us.

Realize that, if a response from another is not love then its fear and they are imprisoned. If your response to another is not love (Love=peace, compassion, joy etc.) then its fear and you're both imprisoned and may not recognize you need each other's help to escape or realize the other preventing your escape and let them go.

This model helped others recognize their source of distress. It was Ricky's father who was his captor. Ricky was struggling with the relationship with his father believing his father abused him as a child, and he was unforgivable. This began to change when he realized his conflicted feelings of being angry with his father and discovering he was projecting it onto others, while at the same time, desiring a close relationship with him.

Ricky, one day, hoped to become a video game designer. While playing one of his games I asked him to explain it to help me understand how he would design a video game. As he explained what needed to happen to get from one level to the next and the challenges involved, I suggested a game based on his struggles with controlling his anger. The challenges he overcame to control his anger would become how to advance from one level to another to win the game. He thought this was a great idea and he began work on this by developing it in a note- book. The types of games he enjoyed and wanted to design called for a hero and a villain. He decided he would be the hero and his father the villain.

As Ricky worked on creating his game, I asked him a question. Did he want to vanquish the villain or redeem him? As it turned out, the underlying question he had to deal with was, did he want to forgive his father or not. He decided his father was unforgivable and as the villain in his game he would be vanquished. I began to notice he started talking to his father differently and with a sense of curiosity. The conflictual nature of their relationship began to diminish, and they began to actually talk. The information he was getting from his father began to replace his false perceptions with the truth he was now learning. The activities around video game development became the process that preceded the PCE.

As his videogame development progressed, resulting in a PCE, after which shifts in perception began to occur, leading to his change of mind and decided the Villain, his father, could be redeemed. With this realization, he admitted his father, could in fact, be forgiven. This gave way to a wider realization of needing to forgive himself to relieve the guilt for the hurt he caused when projecting his rage on to others, leading to even becoming friends with some of those he hurt. This was a significant shift in perception. His episodes of rage dropped from a couple of times a week to none for over 3 months. He still did experience upsets after that, but his anger was greatly diminished, better controlled and manageable and he was able to express himself more appropriately.

Ricky's relationship with his father was his getaway car, and forgiveness, the route Ricky eventually chose to take that gave he and his father a common interest and goal to achieve. That of reconciling the past. We can see how the PCE caused a shift in which Ricky achieved a breakthrough, an insight he didn't have before and changed the course of his life.

All of us are imprisoned by a past that no longer exists. Though the things in our past did occur, it's being unable to let them go that carries the emotions forward allowing the past to keep us in bondage and project it onto others in the present and become the reality we live.

We may feel the distress of fear, anger and guilt due to blaming ourselves or blaming others for what's happening now in our lives but may not recognize the bondage when living it. I certainly didn't when I went through my divorce several years ago when in the grip of the emotions I was going through.

Since then, this model helped others to identify their source of distress. It helped me to recognize the fear of not knowing what change will bring, the anger towards my ex-wife and the guilt of failure, leading up to and through my divorce.

***What he does not realize and needs to learn is that this "self," which can attack and be attacked as well, is a concept he made up*** (25).

This concept is what causes us to see others as our jailors. Because we're conditioned to think, 'If he did it once, he'll do it again,' 'Because it happened before it'll happen again,' regardless of what's happening now. Or, because down through the ages our judgements have assigned characteristics to a particular sex, race or group of people in which social media significantly contributes. The number of social media outlets and availability is mind boggling enough when you consider the contradictions and varying viewpoints adding to the confusion and polarizing opinions on which we base our judgements. How can we always know if the beliefs and opinions we hold are our own, shaping our judgements? Or, are the opinions we hold those of media outlets that have become a part of our everyday life? Or, is it because of long held opinions? 'This is the way it's always been.'

Perceiving in these ways allows us to justify our thinking towards them and even attack, at times as though our survival depended upon it, so our attitude and behaviors become one of defense we call, protecting ourselves, when in fact we made it up.

Thinking this way is a mindset that strongly influence our interactions routinely with others and includes friends, neighbors, husbands, children co-workers and wives, and the list goes on. We are often successful in keeping the past alive by protecting it by projecting it onto others and many times unaware of the source of our distress and from where it originates. Here we can begin to recognize the split mind's dual meaning of fear.

***Judgement is a decision made again and again, against creation and its Creator*** (26).

In this sense, judgement can promote the projection of our fear onto others because we see them as separate, therefore different from us, allowing us to compare ourselves. By comparing ourselves with others we can perceive ourselves to be better, or worse, deserving or undeserving, treated fair or unfairly, and from here, that we're even being attacked, making defense necessary.

This can also work in reverse and not see we are good enough, or as good as others, maybe even feel victimized. We also judge through comparing the past with the present and conclude we may not like someone, some place, or something because of past experiences.

This is a denial of our connectedness to one another and therefore the denial of the source of our oneness. When this happens there can only be fear because of the absence of Love. The absence of Love gives rise to illusions that become the source of our distress that can be projected onto anyone who gives us reminders of our past, regardless of the relationship we have with them.

In Step 2, then, we must identify the source of our distress that has become our prison and see those for who they really are in the present to neutralize them by recognizing they may be just as imprisoned as we and need to be freed, or who may be just trying to help. We can begin to do this by recalling the first memories of the people, places or situation we experienced fear, anger and guilt for the first time.

Are they the same as your most recent experience with these emotions you wrote down earlier in Step 1? Or are they different? If they are different could it be you continue to hold onto those feeling of the past and project them onto the present? If the fear, anger and guilt first experienced and the same people, situation and circumstances are involved, what does this tell you about these relationships now?

# Chapter 5

## Step 3
## Overtake the Warden

Then there's the warden, claiming to be our only friend who won't let us down and tells us we're right and its others who are to blame for our lot in life. They work against us, betray us and can't be trusted. This support provides some degree of comfort to make our stay in captivity more acceptable, even comfortable, which is insane when you think about it. Because we tell this to ourselves the resistance to change is tremendous. The flip side of this, is the warden is not so friendly and attacks our self-image, telling us we deserve what we're going through and deserve the burden of distress we carry. So, to overtake the warden requires awareness that this is the source of illusions and origins of lies we tell ourselves by way of;

**The belief that the self can attack and be attacked;**
**The self is seen as being acted upon by the world;**
**The belief that the world projects its effects on us but in truth:**

**These effects are our projections on the world, therefore, the world we see does not exist** (27). We made it up

This makes the warden...us. We are the ones holding ourselves captive and responsible for our imprisonment by the decisions we make based on our projections.

The most graphic example of this came during a workshop where I met Jimmie. Jimmie shared his periodic bouts with depression in which he rejected activities and people he enjoyed, didn't want to be around anyone, experienced irritability, feelings of sadness and even rejecting God and concluding his depression was the cause. The discussion that followed the presentation of the Fear/Anger/Guilt Model distinguished depression as an effect rather than a cause and the effect was the prison that held him captive. Jimmy readily identified and expressed feeling like a prisoner.

What Jimmie shared with us next took everyone by surprise. He described a reoccurring dream in which he was a prisoner in jail. He described his being brought by guards to the warden's office. When he entered the warden's office the warden was sitting in a swivel chair with his back to him and the guards. Jimmie went on to describe how the warden slowly turned to face them to discover he was the warden he was facing, telling him he was responsible for what he was going through. This was a condition he came to accept, trapping him. He was trapped in what he now began to learn was an illusion that was very real for him.

This is the activity, the ACIM/PP explains, of the ego-mind. The ego-mind is that part of us that battles for control of perceptions which give rise to illusions. The ego is not to be equated with the 'ego' of psychoanalysis that most everyone is familiar, but can be roughly equated with the entire psyche, of which the psychoanalytic 'ego,' gaining notoriety when introduced by Sigmond Freud in the 1920s and 30s, is a part. The ego as the ACIM explains is the belief in the reality of the separated self that stands alone and separate from others and our creator, therefore fosters the belief of attack and defense, protecting itself out of fear, or;

**It is a decision to perceive the universe as you would have created it** (28).

In a follow up discussion a few weeks later Jimmy recalled what happened since the workshop when he felt himself slipping into his all too familiar depression mode. He was clearer about the triggers of his depression when he attempted to reach out to friends, contacting them by phone calls, text and emails and received no response or replies. He began assigning reasons this was happening, coming to the conclusion they didn't care and was angry with them. Instead of turning this anger in on himself resulting in depression, he chose differently this time. When he realized this was his depression trigger, he said he then made a choice to continue to reach out not caring if they responded or not. As he began to connect, what he learned from them was that the reasons they didn't respond, were different than those he assigned to them and really had nothing to do with him. Here was the process preceding the PCE causing a shift in his thinking. As he became aware that the reasons he told himself about why his friends didn't reply were of his own creation was a PCE for him. He realized they were based on his judgements about the others and himself, set in motion by the process began in the workshop preceding his PCE. His shift in perception after the PCE prompted him to choose differently, take different actions and he was able to successfully avoid an episode of depression. Jimmie was quite excited about this new understanding in his journey of self-discovery.

This is the role of the ego-mind, or the warden if we allow it. This was pretty clear in the dreams Jimmy had in which he was the prisoner and the warden. It's that part of us that insist we are right even when the truth is staring us in the face. It is that part of us that makes judgements based on a narrow perspective, or very little information. It is that part of us that would rather be right then happy. It is that part of us that reacts out of fear, disguised as something else and promotes the belief we need to defend ourselves from perceived attacks from others, and attack when feeling threatened because others can't be trusted, proven by our past experiences. These are all included in the ego-mind's thought system that is very difficult to escape and responsible for the distress we experience, which is its aim, and promotes this in others to sustain itself.

## *Produced by fear, the ego reproduces fear* (29)

A lady I met not too long ago, Martha, was experiencing depression that was in some ways, debilitating for her as a result of sexual abuse as a child. She recognized and could identify the Fear/Anger/Guilt Model as her prison. She feared places with a lot of people so ventured very little from home, preventing her from working. It also affected her relationship with her children, especially her teen age daughter. She was surprised to learn many of the problems in their relationship were due to the restrictions and limitations she placed on her oldest daughter out of fear the same thing that happened to her would happen to her daughter. From this Martha realized she was teaching her daughter fear.

She was not only imprisoning herself, but her daughter and her other children, with her restrictions based on the fears she projected onto them. She became the warden who became angry with her daughter when she rebelled against her authority, but to her the restrictions and punishments were out of love. Difficult for her was the admission and acceptance, that she made it up from her fears and imposed a reality on her daughter that her daughter could not see or understand. Starting with her identification with the Fear/Anger/Guilt Model began a process leading to her PCE, which was the realization that she had to teach Love rather than fear. What followed was a shift in her perception motivating her to action to improve her family relationships, desensitize herself to crowds and find work, and after all these years, confront her perpetrator. Martha no longer wanted to accept what she accepted before.

Step 3 is becoming aware that we are the warden who created the illusion of prison for ourselves and others. Go back and view what your most recent experiences with these emotions in Step 1 and listed what would be the origins of these emotions in step 2. Look at the past and the present by looking at Step 1 and 2 from an ego standpoint and the decisions made that contributed to your current circumstances. Now you can decide differently. You can continue old patterns or create new ones. Only you can decide the value in that. In doing so, consider the definition of insanity that most all of have heard before; doing the same thing over and over again and expecting different results.

Awareness of this doesn't always come easy, so help is needed and is made available to us.

# Chapter 6

## Who answers the call for Help?

So, what does it take for someone to "reverse his thinking?" We're told, ***"Sometimes he needs a more structured, extended relationship with an official therapist*** (30), (those who are specifically trained and licensed to perform psychotherapy such as LCSWs, LPCs, LMFTs, psychologist, psychiatrist and others who are licensed in the healing arts of psychotherapy), when situations become severe enough to interfere with our day to day functioning, like some of those mentioned above. However, not everyone needs the services of an official therapist, but because we are all imprisoned in the land of IIL and in need of escape we are provided a way and someone to help as mentioned in the plan.

***'Yet He needs a voice through which to speak His holy Word; a hand to reach His Son and touch his heart.'***

If all are not in need of an official therapist where does the help we need to escape come from? Who is the voice he speaks through? Who is it that extends a helping hand? The ACIM/PP specifically identifies official psychotherapist as those specially trained in the skills, knowledge and methodologies of psychotherapy. This implies there are unofficial psychotherapists with other skill sets. Who are they?

Can you say you have never given help to one who asked? Or, you've never received help when you asked it of someone? Of course the answer would be no. We all have given and received help. When you become aware this, then you not only know who the psychotherapist is, but who is the patient. We are both.

*By whatever route he chooses, all psychotherapy leads to God in the end. We are all His psychotherapist, for he would have us all be healed in Him* (31).

This may seem like an outlandish notion at first. But when you begin to consider what the ACIM tells us about psychotherapy, it begins to make more sense.

In addition to being a psychotherapist I've trained in the martial arts most all my adult life, and many years as a Kung Fu and Tai Chi instructor. I've trained many in both these styles of martial arts over the years. I recall a student of mine some years back. He was a young man in his mid-30s. He became very proficient in Tai Chi and absorbed it like dry ground on a hot day absorbs water. He was my top student. He told me one day of a conversation he had with his father, telling him all about his training and experience in Tai Chi and the benefits to him. His father replied, "Tai Chi is your new religion." It seemed an odd thing to say. Looking back on it now, in this instance the reference is made towards the disciplined, dedicated, practice and devotion to achieve understanding or mastery in a specific area. In this case the learning of Tai Chi. And for many, Tai Chi has become their path to personal growth, discovery and enlightenment. A pathway through which to escape. In this sense, Tai Chi is a form of religious practice.

I mention this to convey an important point put forth in the ACIM/PP.

*To be a teacher of God, it is not necessary to be religious or even believe in God to any recognizable extent* (32).

William James, one of the most respected surveyors of religion, lectured in 1901-2 that, "*the very fact that there are so many and so different from one another is enough to prove that the word 'religion' cannot stand for any single principle or essence, but is rather a collective name.*" (33)

*Religion is experience, psychotherapy is experience. At the highest levels they become one. Neither is truth itself, but both can lead to truth* (34).

Is what William James and ACIM describing here, that our calling, our function, what we do with our life in this world; learn special skills, cultivate talents, and gifts through disciplined practice to a level of mastery, understanding or knowledge gained through training and/or experience, in this sense, religion? And those skills, talents and gifts when used to help another is psychotherapy? These questions may seem ridiculous to many and even be rejected. Before you do, consider this.

*As true religion heals, so must true psychotherapy be religious. Both have many forms, because no good teacher uses one approach to every pupil* (35).

As both have many forms, both have different and varied skills and special knowledge or experience. Or, it could be as simple as helping another with needed information they didn't have or helping them with a task or situation they couldn't do themselves or alone. You may realize from this, times when this has been reversed and we have been the one in need and reached out to another for help because of their skills, profession or knowledge.

The ACIM/PP refers to these folks as unofficial psychotherapists and the one receiving the help, the patient, referring to anyone seeking help from an official or unofficial psychotherapist.

*Either way, the task is the same; the patient must be helped to change his mind about the reality of illusions* (36)

This is the holy interaction that is part of God's plan mentioned earlier, which means, working together to help one another is vital to the plan.

We must recognize that we are all therapist and patient; teacher and student, boss and employee, husband and wife, parent and child, friends, or all of our interpersonal relationships at one time or another and that these roles shift with circumstances, situations and the people involved.

This is what's meant by: *By whatever route he chooses*, for we all have gifts, talents and skills to contribute to help one another, fulfilling our part in the plan.

Those who are trained and have special skills or specialized knowledge, or services are sought after by people in need of them, knowing who they are and how they can help. From what we've learned so far, who is the therapist and who is the patient would be simple to recognize. For others it may be a little more complicated. The roles may not be easily identified as therapist or patient. We may know of them and the form of help they offer, but some will reject it. However, we're told what must happen to start to understand when this happens, begins with;

*Who, then, decides what each brother needs? Surely not you, who do not yet recognize who he is who ask. There is something in him that will tell you, if you listen. And that is the answer; Listen. Do not demand, do not decide, do not sacrifice. Listen* (37).

When you listen and recognize when you're being called on for help, just as official therapists have a psychotherapy skill set to fulfil this function, you as unofficial psychotherapist also have a skill set to fulfill your function. All of you posse and use these skills, maybe even trained in them as part of your chosen profession but may not realize fully their importance to carrying out the plan. These skills are;

- Listening – hear the emotions behind the words.
- Expressiveness (communicate) - the ability to communicate our emotional experience, Love or fear, joy or pain
- Objectivity (suspend judgement) - for you can judge but only the surface and not the depth of the internal condition of people or situations
- Defenselessness - demonstrate that strength lies in defenselessness, not attack
- Forgiveness, which will be addressed in depth later.
- Prayer- psychotherapy is a form prayer
- Healing (not for all, but all can in accordance with their gifts, skills, talents, special knowledge and appropriate experiences)

I lived in the same house for over 30 years, through 2 marriages now. After my second marriage, people told me I needed to sell my house and start anew, but I didn't. But after my last divorce I decided it was time to sell, but the housing crises prevented that from happening by conventional means. I began to feel trapped by memories of the past and the house began to feel like a prison.

Then I looked into finding investors to buy my house for cash. After researching investors, I started getting calls and cards in the mail from investors and investment companies and after talking with many, as far as I was concerned, they wanted me to give them my house for the price of a box of Cracker Jacks and a bag of Skittles.

One day I received a card in the mail from this one investment company. There was something about this one that felt different from the others, so I called and made an appointment. That's when I met Mike.

In getting to know one another somehow, we got into a conversation about religion and our own spiritual growth and we connected. I learned that he became an investor because he wanted to help people in situations such as mine.

He was unable to buy my house for what I wanted but found an investor who would. Though the whole thing he was committed, diligent, encouraging and supportive in his use of many of the skills mentioned earlier, and his special knowledge, that of real estate (religion). He was the therapist and I was the patient. The result of this process (psychotherapy) the house was sold for what I wanted (PCE). I was free and it was the beginning of putting the past in perspective and leaving it behind. Everything changed after that (shift in perception).

Regardless of the help we're given, whether provided by official or unofficial psychotherapists, the process is psychotherapy. ***"For psychotherapy, correctly*** *understood, teaches forgiveness and helps the patient to recognize and accept it* (38).

### 'In such a process, who could not be healed?'

*Psychotherapy is the only form of therapy there is. Since only the mind can be sick, only the mind can be healed. Only the mind is in need of healing* (39). *As all therapy is psychotherapy, so all illness is mental illness* (40).

Psychotherapy is the process that moves us through the steps of the escape plan. If we all must escape and psychotherapy is the process by which we escape, does that mean we all need a psychotherapist? Yes. When circumstances in our lives renders us unable to effectively cope and we struggle from day to day, or we run into a problem we can't solve on our own, yes, we may need to seek out an official therapist. For others no. An unofficial therapist may be all that is needed as discussed earlier. Revisiting this earlier statement now broadens the context and its understanding.

*"By whatever route he chooses, all psychotherapy leads to God in the end. We are all His psycho-therapists, for he would have us all be healed in Him."*

To understand this in the proper context you'll have to first know what is psychotherapy according to the ACIM? *"Psychotherapy is a process that changes the view of the self* (41). *"*

You can see in this how the process preceding a PCE, that begins to change how one sees himself/herself, can be understood as psychotherapy.

The purpose, *"Very simply, the purpose of psychotherapy is to remove the blocks to truth* (42).

The removal of these blocks is the process of psychotherapy that allows one to see the truth of what couldn't be seen before, resulting in a shift in perception including, the view of the self.

*"The process of psychotherapy, then can be defined simply as forgiveness, for no healing can be anything else* (43).

Forgiveness can be the result of a PCE, revealing the need for forgiveness that was blocked from awareness before the shift and presenting the opportunity for us to choose again.

Some of you may think there is no way you could be a psychotherapist, while others of you may think, "I knew it." Think about what you believe a psychotherapist to be. A psychotherapist is someone you form a therapist-patient/client relationship with to help work through problems in situations and relationships that you can't do alone leading to a desirable outcome. What about you? Do you not do this already in your interpersonal relationships with others.

Teacher and student, boss and employer, husband and wife, parent and child, friend and friend or any interaction in which we have received or given help. What this tells us is, it's not a matter of whether you can be a psychotherapist. It's becoming aware you've been one all along and what we've all been doing down through the ages since our earliest ancestors. We have all been therapists and we have all been patients. Just as I am a psychotherapist, but in the relationship with Mike, he was the therapist and I was the patient.

For us to escape the land of IIL we must learn the source of the emotions, fear, anger and guilt, which is almost always people, places or situations from a past that is no more. Included here are those who may serve as a psychotherapist but seen as one of those jailers holding us captive. We may not even like the lesson giver, yet they are there for us, offering they're brand of psychotherapy. That's the thing. We may not realize when facing challenges from others that they may react in such a way that we're unaware of the help being offered because of who is offering and what it is being offered.

You'll recall in the discussion about psychotherapy and religion about how both are experience, are one at the highest levels, have many forms, and no good teacher uses one approach to every pupil. The approach, or brand (religion), of psychotherapy Mike offered was not only desirable, but welcomed. This is not always the case.

*Let us remember, that the ones who come to us for help are bitterly afraid. What they believe will help can only harm; what they believe will harm can only help* (44).

We can believe the illusions are so real that the distress we're experiencing, as painful as it may be, isn't always recognized by us, but recognized by those we have relationships with. We want and try to help, but the one caught in the grip of illusions resist because they don't think they're in need of help and the brand of help we offer falls way short. This happens, I believe, is because the fear from which the illusion is rooted goes unidentified because of the problem behavior that can't be ignored. The process of psychotherapy can certainly help with this and an approach then formulated to address the fear to affect the behavior to reveal the fear. This begins with listening. A skill that's part of the official psycho-therapist, as well as the unofficial psychotherapist skill set.

*On the contrary, he listens patently to each one, and lets him formulate his own curriculum; not the curriculum's goal, but how he can reach the aim it best sets for him* (45)

To show you what I mean, let's take a couple (patients) who are experiencing serious financial struggles and their car breaks down and in need of repair. They take the car to a mechanic (therapist) who evaluates the problem and tells them the cost of the repairs (process of psychotherapy), which is beyond what they can afford.

They argue, blaming each other for their money problems (the illusion), finally asking the mechanic if there was a way he could help them, fearing their financial woes would worsen without their car. He could offer them a discount or work with them in some other way, but that wouldn't solve their financial problems. This is not the brand of psychotherapy he offers.

The mechanic gives them the contact information of an account he uses recommending they see him. When the accountant (therapist) examines their income, expenses and spending habits (process of psychotherapy), it was eye opening for them to see how they mismanaged their finances. The accountant recommends a restrictive budget neither of them liked and resisted at first, but when viewed from the standpoint of their income, expenses and spending habits was the PCE that changed things for them. They understood the value of the restrictive budgeting (the shift), invested in making it work and eventually gained control of their finances, increasing their financial freedom.

This was not an actual situation like the others described along the way, but a composite of many situations I've seen over the years. The purpose is to demonstrate how the therapist/patient relationship, how the process of psychotherapy proceeds the PCE, and the resulting shift in perception when there is resistance by those who don't recognize they need help, or the kind of help that's needed. I also wanted it to be easy and simple to follow to highlight the points made in this section, because sometimes it can be a little more complicated and challenging in real situations. To show you what mean, see if you can recognize the process, the brand, or religion, the

PCE, the psychotherapist and the patient, which will probably be the easiest, and the shift in perception.

Some years back before the pieces of the ACIM started to really come together for me, a mother who brought her 14 year old son, Devon, to see me. He was rather thuggish, rude, disrespectful with a street mentality and generally bad attitude making it clear he didn't want to be there, making me the enemy. His mother was concerned because of the people he was hanging with were a bad influence. He got in fights in school, trouble in the community and had already been involved with the juvenile authorities. He came across as being very angry. His mother was worried he has started down a dark path.

Devon was very resistant during the initial interview and at one point threatened to hurt me if I didn't stop asking questions, as his mother looked on embarrassed and speechless. He didn't seem very committed to the tough guy act he was putting on. He seemed to think his outward expression would be enough to scare me into backing off, indicating to me the presence of fear. He certainly was not ready for traditional psychotherapy, so instead, I wrote an address down and gave it to his mother, while telling Devon that if he wanted a piece of me to be at that address and gave him the date and time. He couldn't back down now and agreed. What he didn't know, was the address he would be coming to was the Kung Fu school where I taught and trained.

In the meantime, I explained to my teacher, Master Wang, what I wanted to do and needed. He told me to use two of our junior black belts who were around Devon's age. I told them what I needed, and they agreed.

On the appointed day and time I was refereeing these two junior black belts in a sparring match when Devon and his mother arrived. They were high kicking, jumping and spinning, really showing off their skills. As Devon looked on, his eyes got really big and he was expressionless. I introduced my junior black belts to Devon and his mother and told him, "If you want a piece of me, you'll have to go through my two junior black belts, then you'll have your shot at me." This is a martial arts tradition. When someone challenges a teacher of his school, the challenger must first defeat the top students to show himself worthy of the opportunity for a "lesson," from the teacher. I told my two students to take him to the dressing room and put Devon in sparring safety equipment and give him tips and pointers about sparring. And they did.

After about 10 minutes they returned, and Devon was fitted in his safety helmet, padded hands, feet and chest protector and the two junior black belts were talking about who would get to spar him first.

He approached and stood on the edge of the training room floor. He then turned and said he didn't want to do this. I had him to repeat this a couple of times, more from shock, I tried to keep hidden, (because I didn't see that coming), than making sure I understood his decision. He didn't change his mind. My two students took him back to the dressing room and got him out of the safety equipment. When he came back, he and his mother left. Before his mother walked out the door, she turned to me gesturing, thank you.

After this I didn't expect to see Devon again. However, he and his mother kept their next appointment the following week. This was surprising enough, but what happened in the meeting was even more surprising. He was different. He was smiling, more engaging and more polite, saying yes sir and no sir. The anger was gone. His mother confirmed the positive changes that have taken place. Over the next couple of meeting with Devon, one of the things he talked about was learning not to judge others, and certainly not threaten someone he didn't know. I was no longer the enemy. After those couple of times I never saw Devon again.

Can you recognize the process (the interaction leading to his decision when he came to the edge of the training room floor), the brand, or religion (martial arts), the PCE (his experience at the martial arts school), the psychotherapist and the patient (the two junior black belts and myself; psychotherapist) and Devon; the patient), which will probably be the easiest, and the shift in perception (his view of himself affecting his attitude and behavior change towards others)? If you did, congratulations! You have skills.

In listening to Devon it was clear, psychotherapy as we know it, was not going to work, so a different brand of psychotherapy with different skills was needed to address his resistance. Devon formulated or chose his own curriculum by way of the threat he made, but not the curriculum's goal, or desired outcome, but how he can reach the aim/goal from the curriculum he chose best sets for him. Fortunately, having another set of psychotherapy skills (martial arts) made the difference for Devon.

And so it is when called on to help another. In both cases, the couple in need of car repair and Devon, we must recognize the limits of the help (skills or special knowledge we have) we can give and direct them to someone who can help or pick up where you left off.

You can understand the significance of this when you think of times when someone has tried to help you and really didn't know enough about the issue you're dealing with to be helpful, either because they just really wanted to help, or thought they were a know-it-all.

To continue the more traditional psychotherapy with Devon would have probably failed after numerous meetings, a lot of talking and his probably refusing any recommendations I'd make. In other words,

***Progress becomes impossible until the patient is persuaded to reverse his twisted way of looking at***

*the world; his twisted way of looking at himself. The truth is simple. Yet it must be taught to those who think it will endanger them. It must be taught to those who will attack because they feel endangered, and to those who need the lesson of defenselessness above all else, to show them what is strength* (46).

It's important to point out the PCE is the outcome sought from the psychotherapy process because it facilitates change by way of a shift in perception. What is illustrated with Devon is that the PCE can be instantaneous compared to the process preceding it.

How many times have you tried to help someone by talking to them in hopes of 'reversing their twisted way of looking at the world and their twisted way of looking at himself,' and met with resistance? This is particularly frustrating when it is someone you're close to and care about. Then some outside force (unofficial psychotherapy / psychotherapist) intervenes that provides an experience or event (PCE) and a shift occurs and changes things, sometimes in unexpected ways for that person. I believe the chances of this happening is higher for those unofficial therapists with specific skills, gifts, talents and special knowledge who extend help to those who don't need the help of an official psychotherapist. I believe this is what's meant by;

*What is the need for sickness then? Given this simple shift, all else will follow. There is no need for complicated change. There is no need for long analyses and wearying discussions and pursuits. The truth is simple, being one for all* (47).

Whether official or unofficial psychotherapist, or patient, we have a better understanding of the role we play in this escape plan, the scope of the process it entails that the ACIM calls psychotherapy. One of the most important points of identifying who the helpers are is that we are equipped in our own way to help each other, making escape possible for all. This brings us to the next step.

# Chapter 7

## Step 4
## Secure a Getaway car

***Relationships are still the temple of the Holy Spirit***
(48), tells us we cannot escape alone and must take
someone with us. We must help others to escape and
escape together through the relationships we form,
develop and cultivate.

This means relationships become our getaway cars.
Relationships provide the means for escape by
showing us our projections of the past onto the
present, reevaluate it, giving us the opportunity, for
both therapist and patient, to decide again. In
psychotherapy this is called transference.

It is where the individual transfers feelings and
attitudes from a person or situation in the past on to
a person or situation in the present and where the
process is likely to be, at least to some degree,
inappropriate to the present situation. This
transference can be positive or negative depending

on the past experience being projected from the past onto the present person or situation.

In an article by Gladeana McMahon. A psychologist from the UK, she explains transference.

*Transference is seen as being a general phenomenon and for those who believe in its existence is one that is acted out by everyone and often contributes to the decisions we make about those we chose as friends and partners as well as towards those we may not like without that person doing anything other than being him or herself.*

People sometimes know when this is happening. Many times they don't. We may experience being treated badly by someone and not have a clue as to why when we become the object of their transference. They may not know either. This is an illusion. But if they can say they treated you the way they did because of how they were treated in their past, it could change things for the better when you both no longer have to deal with the illusion this created.

What is not easily recognized, sometimes not even by trained psychotherapist, is what is called counter transference. With a counter transference, things could go a different way.

*When client/patient/or people we interact with responds to you in a particular way you may find yourself responding back to the way s/he is treating you. In this case the term Counter Transference is used to describe the unconscious feelings you may experience towards them based on the way they're acting towards you. Again this could either be a positive or negative Counter Transference (49).* What do transference and counter transference mean?

It means we see the negative treatment we receive from others as an intentional attack rather than the illusion created from the other's past. Often, we ourselves have treated others from a past that is no more, but don't recognize these unconscious negative memories or feelings superimposed onto the present.

When we do recognize transference or counter transference in our relationship(s), and that we are either the patient or therapist, it becomes an opportunity for both to decide differently. We can respond in kind because of our own past, counter transference, and promote the illusion of another, or choose not to and choose differently about the other and our self. This is what's meant by;

**The therapist sees in the patient all that he has not forgiven in himself and is thus given another chance to look at it, open it to reevaluation and forgive it** (50).

Psychotherapy, then can provide the opportunity for both therapist and patient to reconcile the perceptions, or illusions brought about by negative transference and counter transference. This is what makes relationships the ideal getaway car for our escape.

This could not be made clearer than in the ACIM workbook, lesson 192. *"Who could be set free while he imprisons anyone? A jailer is not free, for he is bound together with his prisoner. He must be sure that he does not escape, and so he spends his time in keeping watch on him. The bars that limit him becomes the world in which his jailer lives, along with him. And it is on his freedom that the way to liberty depends for both of them."*

For Debbie, Ricky and the others mentioned, their getaway cars were those they were in relationships with they felt were their captors, holding them hostage. They came to learn how they viewed those who were their jailers were based on projections from their past, so were not real, but were made real by the belief in their perceptions.

One example of how this plays out and transference and countertransference was a dimension of releasing the past from which illusions were created was the case with the young mother, Maria and her son Jeremy. Having already been diagnosed with ADHD and struggling to manage his impulsive and hyperactive behavior, and feared herself becoming a bad mother, causing Jeremy to not love her. As it turns out, as a child her experience was similar to Jeremy's and identified strongly with what he was going through that governed how she dealt with him. The transference.

It was when she began seeking help for Jeremy, did she learn she too was dealing with undiagnosed ADHD as a youth. She tried dealing with Jeremy's behavior in ways she was dealt with by her parents when growing up, making her aware of how much she got away with then, when those methods from her past didn't work with Jeremy now. Out of frustration and anger she tried becoming tougher. Jeremy would rebel, throw terrible tantrums and she would feel sorry for him, give in, deepening her guilt, so by the time we met she was very distraught. This transference left her feeling trapped, like an inadequate parent and imprisoned by the dynamics of the relationship with her son.

By guiding and teaching her in the development of a token economy the relationship that developed between us at times was that of teacher and student. On a few occasions, Maria referred to my role as like an uncle, which I took to mean as sort of a parental figure. This was an indication that transference was in play. I used her interpretation of my role to my advantage, providing support, direction and skills training in a parental, yet professional fashion. This was the countertransference from which she learned to better manage his behavior using the token economy as a tool. With emphasis on the discipline and patience she needed to make the token economy work, her confidence in her parenting improved as did her self-esteem. Their relationship became the vehicle, aiding in her escape from the distressful emotions holding them both captive by the beliefs she held about herself. In a few months she was better able to deal with Jeremy's behavior in a firm, yet positive manner and their relationship improved.

The ACIM tells us that when escaping illusions things don't necessarily change, but how we view them, or a change in perception does, allowing us to make different choices. When reviewing Jeremy's progress after a few months his mother found Jeremy's behavior had progressed very little.

However, her ability to manage his behavior had drastically improved. Due in part to positive counter transference, the tools and skills gained through the process provided, the learning and implementing of a token economy, but largely due to the PCE, her discovery of the progress she made, and the shift in perception that followed that changed the way she perceived herself.

This further illustrates from our earlier discussion about the Warden that;

*These effects are our projections on the world. Therefore, the world we see does not exist.* We made it up.

Recognizing transference and countertransference in relationships can be another way to recognize illusions. Another and more personal example occurred with Debbie when her ex-husband joined her in one of our meetings. Not only did I become aware of the transference, after witnessing their interaction, but something else happened as well. I became aware of my own counter transference as I was going through relationship struggles of my own that eventually led to my divorce. I became aware of emotions and behavior in my own relationship that began a shift in my thinking.

She had given me another chance to look at it, open it to re-evaluation and forgive it. Though it took some time after the divorce, my ex-wife and I could talk about what went wrong, we came to the conclusion that we should have never gotten married as we were better friends, which was now the goal we both agreed on. The countertransference I experienced played an important part in the process to reach this place with my ex-wife.

In looking back, through this process we were both therapist and patient. Our relationship had become the getaway car we both needed to release the past and begin to heal.

*Each patient who comes to a therapist offers him a chance to heal himself. He is therefore his therapist. And every therapist must learn to heal from each patient who comes to him. He thus becomes his patient* (51).

All cultures including ours could not function without relationships from the smallest, making brief eye contact and connecting with a stranger, to close personal relationships, to international relationships on a global scale. When you find yourself in a situation when you are the therapist, called on for help; whether you're asked to head up a project at work, respond to a friend asking for help or your husband had a bad day at work, here's the most important part of this escape plan and why relationships, as our getaway cars are so important.

All of our relationships have the potential for helping us to escape, because we're all either therapist or patient engaged in the process of psychotherapy. If we can accept this, then we can understand that our mental and even physical distress is the product of our illusions for which we are all in need of psychotherapy.

Our recognition of this can relieve us of the projections, transference, counter transference, and the distress they can cause and put the past in prospective, allowing healing to take place.

In Step 4 we identify and re-evaluate our relationships, regardless of the type, and recognize when we are therapists or patient and use the skills identified for relationship growth, success and/or escape. As we cannot escape alone and must take others with us along the way, recognize then, that those we're in relationships with will be our getaway cars, the means of escape, and/or success. Have you listed them earlier as jailers or captors responsible for imprisoning you? Can you tell when your role in a relationship is therapist of patient? Are there new relationships not of your past, but of your future? Don't overlook those relationships that are loving, supportive, uplifting and have a positive influence on your life, as getaway cars. Which skills will help you make these relationships work better for you?

## Chapter 8

### Step 5
### Map out and be certain of your escape route

Now that you have begun to recognize those people and situations for who and what they are they don't have the power over you they once did. The shrinking influence of the warden's illusions allows you to begin to see those you believed were jailers were offering help or asking for help, as unpleasant as it may feel at the time. This realization maps out the certainty of the escape route...forgiveness.

*What must the teacher do to ensure learning? What must the therapist do to bring healing about? One thing is required and asked of everyone.*

And that is, *each one must share one goal with someone else, and in doing so, lose all sense of separate interest* (52).

This is one of the more challenging parts of the escape plan. Becoming aware that you were the warden all along and forgiving yourself and those people and the situations involved.

The escape route then, is forgiveness for it provides many opportunities for forgiveness by first becoming aware of your interactions in your relationship with others, if you're the therapist or the patient, teacher or student, employer or employee, parent of child, giving help or asking for help, directly or indirectly.

Second, begin to notice that all interactions are relationships, whether a brief encounter or committed, long term relationships. Recognize it as therapist/patient relationship and which are you. This can often give us the opportunity to forgive and be forgiven, see things differently, decide differently, and see yourself (change view of self ACIM/PP.2.2.1.4) differently apart from what your past of being trapped in the land of IIL would have you believe. The opportunity for forgiveness is most apparent after the shift caused by a PCE.

Forgiveness, as mentioned above is the more challenging part of the escape plan. Admitting our responsibility, that we could be wrong is not supported by the Warden, for the belief is, control would be lost, and we'd be defenseless. The Warden would have us believe this is a bad thing, but without the illusions what is the need for defense?

The difficulty is allowing ourselves to be defenseless, believing it to be weakness or making us vulnerable, rather than a strength. I learned of this firsthand after going through my divorce. Though it wasn't easy for my ex-wife and I, we had to accept one another for who we were. By allowing ourselves to drop our defenses and accept our responsibilities for what happened that got us here and forgive each other, could the healing begin for the outcome of remaining friends be achieved. Both being veterans of divorce this would be a first for us both.

This escape route is created by forgiveness mentioned earlier. Forgiveness is healing, which is the aim of psychotherapy.

What does this healing involve?

**Fear-** Reconsider the causes of fear and learn to evaluate fear correctly (53)

**Anger-** The belief that attack is protecting ourselves; to whatever extent we come to realize that this is an error, to that extent we are truly saved (54).

**Guilt-** Relieve the mind of the insane burden of guilt it carries so wearily, and healing is accomplished (55)

In those conversations with my ex wife we were both therapist and patient, giving us both the opportunity to forgive the fear anger and guilt we both experienced and begin healing, giving each other the chance to escape our past and begin anew.

***This must be the teaching, if his lesson is to be that sanity is safe*** (56)

Through this process we can learn the great power we posse and come to understand that if we created the reality that got us this far, we have the power to create the reality we want going forward when we learn the value of forgiveness.

This is how the process of psychotherapy works. Teach forgiveness and forgiveness strengthens relationships. This was a powerful lesson for those discussed who were experiencing the emotional distress imprisoning them. They discovered they preferred a positive relationship rather than being imprisoned by illusions, and for me, by learning the power of forgiveness promotes healing and can be life changing.

In Step 5 our escape route is forgiveness. This includes ourselves. The escape route of forgiveness allows us to dissolve the past into the proper perspective. We must keep in mind that forgiveness is not a quick fix. Forgiveness is a process. Reverend Sheila Gautreaux provides us with some insight into forgiveness, along with an affirmation that can be helpful in the forgiveness process. The four quick steps and the guidelines for living forgiveness can assist us along our escape route. It is a necessary skill whether therapist or patient.

CONCEPT:

To discover how to live without criticism, condemn-nation or judgement of self or others; to choose to see the perfection in everything; to practice forgiveness moment by moment; and live in the present moment without reference to the past or future.

SCRIPTURE:

Luke 23:34 Jesus said, "Father forgive them, for they do not know what they are doing." And they divided up his clothes by casting lots.

METAPHYSICS:

FORGIVE- To give up the false for the Truth (Fillmore, Revealing Word)

They Know Not What They Do – They are not aware of the Truth of God – The Universal Laws that govern our thoughts and actions; Consciousness

FOUR (4) QUICK STEPS TO FORGIVENESS:
1. WOW! Look what I created.
2. I notice my feelings and my judgements.
3. I am willing to see the perfection in this situation
4. I choose the power of peace

GUIDELINES FOR LIVING FORGIVENESS
1. Heal/forgive the past by forgiving everything – even those things you believe are unforgivable: Forgiveness is the gift we give ourselves.
2. Practice mindfulness – stay in the present moment.
3. Remember God never forgives – God never held it against us in the first place.

4. God is pure Love. God does not punish; we punish ourselves when we falsely believe we are separate from God.

5. Every attack is a call for love. Hurt people, hurt people. They have misplaced their identity.

6. We are made in the image and likeness of God; therefore, we are pure Love and cannot be otherwise unless we have spiritual amnesia.

7. TO FORGIVE IS TO LIVE!

AFFIRMATION:

I AM WILLING TO LET GO AND LET GOD. I AM WILLING TO SEE THE PERFECTION IN EVERYTHING. I AM WILLING TO FORGIVE

"Living forgiveness-WOW! LOOK WHAT I CREATED "by Reverend Sheila Gautreaux
Unity of Houston

**Chapter 9**

**Step 6**
**You'll need an expert and experienced getaway driver and guide you can trust to navigate your escape safely.**

Who is this driver?

Here's the most important step of our escape plan and why relationships, as our getaway cars are necessary. When we come together in a common goal or interest, no matter what it is, we join with others and share that common goal, that idea, or how to get things done and work together at the exclusion of self-interest. It's the joining of minds that share an idea, a vision, that bring it into manifestation. Whether it be the mother and father of a family who stuck by their son who struggled in school and got him back on the right track or a board of directors all deciding on what will improve their company. It is this joining, this team work that cannot fail to lead to success because, there is a true one that never fails to appear to be our getaway driver and guide.

You may refer to him as your subconscious mind, that Voice, that feeling, Intuition, Master Mind, Devine Mind, or whatever you want to call it matters not, but remember, relationships are the temple of the Holy spirit and if relationships are our getaway cars then who else could this driver and guide be?

Mike and my ex-wife were the first 2 of many getaway cars that got me this far. There will be many relationships that will be getaway cars along our escape route and some of them will call for forgiveness, especially if any were seen as jailers that now become our getaway cars.

It is this joining in relationships that cannot fail to lead to success.

*If any two are joined, He must be there. It does not matter what their purpose is, but they must share wholly to succeed. It is impossible to share a goal not blessed by Christ...*(57)

Joining may mean stepping into another's fear with them and becoming their getaway car as a first step to helping them escape. Said another way, you may have to sometimes break into prison to be with them to expose their nightmarish illusions for what they are and guide to them, showing them the way to escape.

I mentioned earlier that when I learned to step aside things would happen that surprised even me.

This brings me to Carl, a 10 year, who recently lost his mother, but had not begun the grieving process. His behavior became a problem. There was information Carl did not have about the death of his mother. For him the withholding of information meant there was something to fear, so became fearful himself. His fear was not only expressed as anger, but in the form of a monster that appeared in his dreams a few times a week. I explained to Carl this sometimes happens when fears are kept locked away in a little box deep inside us. I asked Carl to draw a picture of this monster and bring it with him next time. He brought the picture and when I looked at his monster, asked him if the monster said anything. He told me he only made sounds like, Grrrrrrr. That's when I heard myself ask him, how did he know this was not a message. My question shocked me but didn't seem to shock Carl as he answered, I don't know. Again, I heard myself ask, don't you think you should find out? I was once again surprised but, he agreed.

I wasn't prepared for what happened next. When he came back next time and I asked if the monster showed up. He told me the monster came the night before. When asked what happened Carl explained he listened to the growls and it was a message. The message was for him to open the box and let the fear out. As I listened as Carl talked about this and how the monster wasn't real and he made it up. I just looked at him in astonishment. That was the last visit he had from the monster. This just demonstrates what can be overcome when two minds come together in a common interest.

Stepping into this with him, our relationship became the getaway car he needed to help him escape.

During a family meeting the information surrounding his mother's death was revealed. Forgiveness and grieving were now common goals of the family relationships. A Burning Bowl ritual seem to be an appropriate way to bring forth the getaway car driver to help Carl and his family initiate the grieving process and rebuild family relationships. And it was.

*Be thankful, therapist, that you can see such things as this, if you but understand your proper role* (58).

My intention with the illustrations in each of the 6 stages was not the technique or methods used, but to demonstrate that it doesn't matter. It's the process, we know as psychotherapy, and the particular talents, skills and gifts, or just the desire to help another obtain that shift caused by a PCE that's important. Whether your role is psychotherapist, realtor, secretary, accountant, maintenance person, politician, mechanic or martial arts instructor. It matters not.

*One asks for help; another hears and tries to answer in the form of help. This is the formula for salvation, and must heal* (59).

What matters is when someone comes to us or we seek help from another, we are where we're supposed to be and all we need do is trust in the plan and follow the steps. We need one another if we're to escape the Land of IIL and this is the plan given us to do so.

*No one is healed alone. This is the joyous song salvation sings to all who hear its Voice* (60).

Now you understand the importance of relationships and the joining necessary to help each other through this process. We are that voice saving each other from illusions, and when we do, we save ourselves because no one is healed alone.

Next stop. Freedom

Step 6 is identifying who we need to join with to resolve a problem, situation or work towards an agreed upon goal. When we join with another in a common goal, we can accomplish more than we can alone and can now begin to see the reality at the end of the illusions. Do you know who you will join with to escape?

## Chapter 10

### Step 7
### Know your destination, where you are escaping to?

*All blocks to the remembrance of God are forms of unforgiveness, and nothing else. The world has marshalled all its forces against this one awareness, for in it lies the ending of the world and all it stands for* (61).

When we can grasp this awareness fully, we can decide we want something different, and that we can create the reality we want, comes the dawning that our escape literally brings the ending of the world and all it stands for.

I was struck with a fuller understanding of this on my birthday in November 2018 when I realized the impact of the last 3 years.

My marriage came to an inevitable end in mid-2016. The struggles between my wife and I worsened, but a part of me held onto the notion that something would happen that would turn things around, while another part of me knew things were headed toward an inevitable end. The bit of hope I had was offset by the need to emotionally protect myself. I did this by throwing myself into my work. I was clinical director of a new mental health company early in its infancy.

Submerging myself in helping to grow this company seemed to be just what I needed at first to distract myself from the emotional distress of what was happening in my life. As the company grew with more staff, more clients and more complex systems to manage it all, it began to add to my distress with more demands on my time and energy.

Stress relieve for me was my martial arts training. Time for this got harder and harder to find. It wasn't just because of the demands made on my time, but the pain from an arthritic hip was making it harder to be motivated to train with the time I did have as the pain was becoming harder to endure.

After the divorce I found myself without a support network, which is how it goes many times after a divorce, friends go with one or the other, or many were married and living their life. And who wants to be a third wheel? Selling my house and moving to another part of town also played a role in being unable maintain a support system.

Due to the demands of my job, in which a lot of work was done at home, or driving to the home of clients, my attendance at church virtually dropped out. I relied on prayer, meditation and church tv.

After my divorce became final and moving into my apartment, it was November 2016 when my daughter, Tina, texted me, asking what I was going to do for Thanksgiving. When I told her nothing, which was the same answer I gave her when she asked what I was going to do for my birthday a couple of weeks before, she texted me back with an emoticon so sad my phone started to cry.

It made me realize how alone I felt, and she seemed to understand that. I guess I was aware that the isolation I was experiencing was self-imposed. I've heard this said about Scorpios. When hurt and in pain we withdraw from the world to heal our wounds. This certainly seemed to be the case.

Skip a head to November 2018. When in meditation one evening, what came to me was; I bring the end of the world. I was like, what? What does that mean? Don't go, tell me more. I got no answer right away. I couldn't see it at the time, but my world as I knew it was coming to an end.

Over the past couple of years, I got to know a wonderful woman and she threw a birthday party for me and invited all my friends. When we all came together to celebrate my birthday, I looked around and the answer came. Except for my other daughter, Toni, no one there I knew 2 years before. A PCE was underway.

When I took a step back for a wider view of the past 2 years, I became aware I was in a new relationship with the most magnificent woman and I had new friends. I had a new best friend who was sometimes a little sister, sometimes a big sister and all the time a good friend. We were business partners, along with another who since has become a good friend, in a new mental health company, Fresh Start Therapeutic Services. In 2017 I had hip replacement surgery and once again I could continue training in the martial arts. I lived in a new place, I was a member in a new Unity church close to home and in a course in Miracles group for the first time.

The world I knew and all it stood for had ended. The message received in meditation seemed to signal my world was coming to an end, leading to my birthday party that turned out to be a PCE. This was followed by a shift in perception that brought the realization and appreciation of being happy, of experiencing Love once again.

It's one thing to help others through this process. I could step back with a degree of objectivity, but it's quite another when you live it and feel all the emotions, moving from one step to another and really understand what escape from the Land of IIL is like and what it really means. A chance at life you didn't think you had before.

Our escape destination, as Marrianne Williamson tells us, is A Return to Love, from her book of the same name. The outcome is the same for us all, but the destination is different for everyone and reflected in the lives we live.

When we are living the life we Love it can become like Heaven on earth. Are you living the life you Love? Picture in your mind what the life you love looks like.

What would it take for that picture in your mind to become the reality you live?

Who are those who could help? What actions can be taken to bring about this new and preferred reality?

Notice the thoughts that come about when picturing your new reality. They are not all for your success. If they were, you'd be living the life you love.

At a Dream Builder workshop, Mary Morrissey told a story of a woman out jogging and began thinking of a way to become very successful in her business. Without being aware, the voice of her past slipped in, telling her she couldn't do it, why it was a bad idea and why it wouldn't work. When she became aware of what was happening, she stopped and said to herself,

EXCUSE ME!
I interrupt this broadcast with an important message from my soul. I am a child of God and I DESERVE to live a life I love living.

This declaration was the opening of a very powerful workshop experience that dramatized what we tell ourselves based on what the world would have us believe about who we are, then create illusions that make it so.

By removing the blocks to forgiveness and seeing illusions for what they are, we can change our minds about it and decide what we want instead, and literally set a new course and create the life we love.

Don't allow the Land of IIL to be the place that your dreams come to die, for this process, this activity of psychotherapy, I've learned by helping others, and living it myself, is the source of Miracles.

In the end, it comes down to one thing, we are love and the only place to escape to while we're here, is a life we love to live. The destination you choose awaits you and the miracles you seek to take you there. Isn't it time you live the life you want to love and love the life you're living?

## About the author

Ed holds a, Master of Science in Social Work –
MSSW degree the UT Arlington, Graduate School
of Social Work, a Licensed Clinical Social Worker
in Texas and a member of National Association of
Social Workers.

As a psychotherapist Ed has made a career of
helping those wanting to improve or maintain their
mental health and have a better life.

When he discovered A Course in Miracles early in
his career, it has had a growing influence in his
approach to psychotherapy and the importance of
understanding and addressing our spiritual nature as

a strength and resource to solving the problems we face in this world.

This book is about what Ed learned from viewing A Course in Miracles from a psychotherapist perspective. His hope is that readers benefit from what he shares in his book, Escape from Insanity, Illusions and Lies

Escape from Insanity, Illusions and Lies is Ed's first book published in September 2019

## Index of references

1. ACIM/PP.2.lV.3.9

2. ACIM/PPPP Inro.1.1

3. The Light of Christ Truth;

http://lightofchristtruth.com/Enl_spirituality/Course-in-Miracles.html

4. Foundation for inner peace website https://peoplepill.com › people › helen-schucman

5. ACIM/PP.2.lV.7.10

6. Question on the death of r.Schucman; KenWapnick

https://www.reddit.com/r/ACIM/comments/pki0w/question_on_the_death_of_dr_schucman/

7. ACIM/PP.2.lV.1.9

8. ACIM/PP.2. ll.1.6

9. ACIM/PP.2. V.5.12

10. ACIM/PP.1.1.1.2

11. ACIM/PP.2.2.1.4

12. ACIM/PP.2.lV.1.9

13. ACIM/PP.2.lV.2.9

14. ACIM/PP.1.1.4.2

15. Oct 27, 2017 What Happens in the Brain When We Feel Fear | Science (15) Oct 27, 2017 What Happens in the Brain When We Feel Fear | Science | Smithsonian https://www.smithsonianmag.com/science.../what-happens-brain-feel-fear-180966992/

16. https://kidshealth.org/en/teens/phobias.html

17. Compassionate Being   https://www.tranquilfreedom.com

18. Eugene H. Merrill in his article, Entry into Fear https://www.biblestudytools.com/dictionaries/bakers-evangelical-dictionary/fear.html

19. From Wikipedia, the free encyclopedia

20. GotQuestions.org

21. Bishop  Arthur J. Serratelli- The Fear of the Lord: A Biblical Understanding  -  https://bishopserratelli.rcdop.org/news/the-fear-of-the-lord-a-biblical-understanding

22.  ACIM/CHAPTER  2/THE  SEPARATION  AND  THE ATONEMENT/Fear and Conflict

23. ACIM/Chapter 29.2.606

24. ACIM/PP.2.lV.7.10

25. ACIM/PP.1.1.3.2

26. ACIM/PP.2.lV.1.9

27. ACIM/PP.1.1.4.2

28. ACIM/PP.2.lV.1.9

29. ACIM.7.VI.4.124

30. ACIM/PP Intro 1.1

31. ACIM/PP.1.1.5.3

32. ACIM/PP.2. ll.1.6

33. The Varieties of Religious Experience: A study in Human Nature by William James

34. ACIM/PP.2. ll.2.6

35. ACIM/PP.2. ll.7.7

36. ACIM/PP.Intro.1.1

37. ACIM/PP.3. l.2.18

38. ACIM/PP.1.1.2.2

38. ACIM/PP.1.1.2.2

40. ACIM/PP.2.lV.1.9

41. ACIM/PP.2.2.1.4

42. ACIM/PP.1.1.1.2

43. ACIM/PP.2.VI.1.13

(44) ACIM/PP.2. V.2.12

45) ACIM/PP.2. V.2.12

46) ACIM/PP.2.lV.11.11

(47) ACIM/PP.2.lV.11.11

48. ACIM/PP.2. ll.1.6

49. Written by Gladeana McMahon in Coaching Tools

50. ACIM/PP.2.Vl.6.15

51) (ACIM/PP.2.Vll.1.15)

(52) (ACIM/PPPP.2. ll.8.7)

53) (ACIM/PP.1.1.1.2)

54) (ACIM/PP.2.2.1.4)

55. ACIM/PP.2.lV.11.11

56. ACIM/PP.2.lV.10.11

57. ACIM/PP.2. ll.6.7

58. ACIM/PP.2.Vll.9.17

59. ACIM/PP.2.lll.3.8

60. ACIM/PPPP.2.Vl.7.15

61. ACIM/PP.2. ll.3.6

Made in the USA
Coppell, TX
17 December 2019